GRANDPA'S DEER STORY

J. William Zoldak

Illustrations by Misti Feliciano Hobbs

Dedication

Dedicated to my wife Laura C. Zoldak (Grandma).

Grandpa's Deer Story

J. William Zoldak

FIRST EDITION

Hardcover ISBN: 978-1- 948018-82-1
Softcover ISBN: 978-1- 948018-83-8

ALL RIGHTS RESERVED.

©2020 J. William Zoldak
Illustrations by Misti Feliciano Hobbs.
Deer photo © Robmckay

No part of this publication may be translated, reproduced or transmitted in any form without prior permission in writing from the publisher.

STONEHEDGES

Published by Stonehedges
OXFORD, MASSACHUSETTS

Dear Grandchildren,

Today I want to tell you a story about an experience I had a long time ago with some white tail deer. It happened near my childhood home along the west side of the Hudson River in the town of Cornwall, New York (about 60 miles north of New York City). White tail deer are wonderful and fascinating animals that are today very common and almost tame in some areas, but when I was a boy, there were far fewer of them, and they were quite wild.

The house I lived in at this time was located about a quarter of a mile off a main road in a very rural section of town surrounded by small family farms. Behind my house, separated by a stone wall, was a five-acre pasture. In the center of this pasture was a very large Ash tree. During warm summer days, cows would often graze in this pasture and relax in the shade of this beautiful tree. Beyond the pasture was an alfalfa field separated from the pasture, not only by another stone wall, but also by a thick growth of small trees and brush that lined the edge of the field and often referred to as a hedge row. The alfalfa grass had been hayed off in June, and since this story takes place in late summer, the alfalfa had grown back. The deer particularly liked feeding in this field. Beyond the alfalfa field was a large wooded area containing a full spectrum of forest vegetation and wildlife, including a large herd of white tail deer.

Often just before dusk, deer would cautiously come out of the woods and graze on the alfalfa. Because the alfalfa field sloped toward my house and the hedge row between the pasture and that field had some sparse places in it, I could see the deer from my house. One evening as I watched the deer from my back yard, I got to wondering how far I could sneak up on them before scaring them off. The more I thought about it, the more interested I became until I finally decided to give it a try. Using the denser parts of the hedge row to shield myself from the deer, I crossed the pasture without being detected. Then, hiding behind the stone wall at the edge of the alfalfa field, I watched the deer as they ventured further and further out into the open. There were six deer grazing fairly close together near the back part of the field.

As I watched them, I thought about something I learned from either my father or my grandfather (I don't remember which). If you stayed down wind of the deer so they could not pick up your scent and you were perfectly still, the deer would not be alarmed even if they could see you. Well, I decided to put this theory to the test. The evening was clear and comfortably mild with a slight breeze which, by luck, was blowing toward me. The conditions seemed perfect for the experiment.

As I surveyed the surroundings, I looked for potential obstacles to my plan, such as a chatty bird that might give me away (crows and blue jays are particularly troublesome in this regard) or a small mammal, such as a squirrel, that might sound the alarm. Seeing no problems, I slowly crawled over the stone wall moving only when the deer lowered their heads to graze or when they were looking in a different direction. They seemed very content gorging themselves on the sweet alfalfa grass.

On the other side of the wall, I slowly and cautiously stood up and waited to see if I had been detected. They stayed in place seemingly unalarmed. Waiting until they were calmly grazing, I slowly took a step forward and, again, there was no noticeable alarm in their movement. So, I again waited until they were preoccupied with the alfalfa and then took another step forward. I did this several more times until I was clearly out in the field where the deer could easily see me. To my surprise there was no concern on their part at all. I took a few more steps to within, perhaps, 50 feet of the nearest deer. I was feeling pretty good about my success so far, and I would have been quite content if it had ended at this point, but it didn't.

The sun by now was close to the horizon, and daylight was fading. I could see my shadow on the ground which made me wonder if the deer would pick up any movement in that shadow. I didn't have much time, however, to ponder this thought because just then the deer that was closest to me seemed to become aware of my presence. She was a large, beautiful adult deer known as a doe. She had big brown eyes, a brown coat, and a snowy white belly. Her ears were bent forward trying to detect any sound, her nose was in the air sniffing the wind, and her white tail twitched nervously. I had been discovered! Remaining perfectly still, I waited for her to make the next move. I didn't have to wait long. She began slowly and deliberately taking steps toward me, each one measured and with caution.

As I remained statue-like, the other deer all stopped grazing and devoted their full attention to the drama that was unfolding before them. Step by step she moved ever closer with all parts of her body on full alert. After every few steps, she would back track a little and then come forward again. Sometimes she would move to the left or to the right and then advance forward once more. When she was about 10 feet away, she stopped and looked straight at me as she twitched her ears and sniffed the air trying to figure me out. I, on the other hand, was locked in place breathing as little as possible. We remained like this for what seemed like an eternity but was probably only moments. Then with her head lowered, ears forward, nose sniffing, and her eyes fixed on me, she moved ever closer until she was only a couple of feet away. By then I was holding my breath, realizing that I was in one of those moments in life that only happens once.

She took one more step, stretched her neck, and laid her cold, moist nose on the back of the hand at my side. The moment her nose touched my hand she made a backward lunge and a loud snort. She then darted toward the woods as fast as she could run. The other deer, who had been watching, took off with her… Within an instant, the drama was over and I was standing in the field alone.

Well, grandchildren, I have two thoughts that I hope you take away from this story. First, I want you to think about how brave this deer was to venture forward while knowing that danger was near her all the while. Remember that courage is not restricted to humans alone. The other thought that I want you to think about is that there will be cherished moments in your lives that you carry with you forever. Of these moments, I wish you many.

Love as always,

Grandpa

THE END

White Tail Flags

White tail deer are graceful and timid animals that are widespread across America.

They live in almost any place there are fields, meadows, or woodlands.

Their diet is made up of mainly grasses and other vegetation found in their environment.

In the fall of the year, they browse the forest floor looking for acorns to munch on. Acorns are like candy to deer.

They spend their entire lives close to the place they are born.

Adult male deer are called bucks. Buck deer have antlers that fall off in late winter and grow back during the spring and summer. The antlers are covered with velvet at first, but lose that outer coating as they age.

Adult female deer are called does. Does give birth in the spring time to small spotted babies called fawns. The fawns lose their spots as they age toward adulthood.

Although deer can be seen anytime of the day, they are most active at night searching for food when there is less activity in their surroundings.

Just after dawn, they often bed down in a hiding place where they remain during the daylight hours.

Dawn and dusk are the best times to catch a glimpse of them as they transition in their routine.

Throughout history, deer numbers have fluctuated depending upon environmental conditions such as the number of predators (including humans) near where they live.

The name white tail deer comes from the fact that they have a large white tail that stands straight up when they run, often referred to as a flag. Humans may see only those flags during sightings.

Mule deer (the other major species of deer in America) are similar but larger, with bigger ears, and no white tail. They are found mainly in the western states.

www.ingramcontent.com/pod-product-compliance
Lightning Source LLC
Chambersburg PA
CBHW051404110526
44592CB00023B/2951